How to Make Smoothies!

Elena Martin

www.Rigby.com
1-800-531-5015

We like to make smoothies.

You can make smoothies, too.

Fill a cup with juice.

Put it in the blender.

Fill a cup with yogurt.

Put it in the blender.

Fill a cup with fruit.

Put it in the blender.

Fill a cup with ice.

Put it in the blender.

Cut up a banana.

Put it in the blender.

RRRRRRR!

Everything gets mixed up.

Everything gets smooth.
This will be yummy!

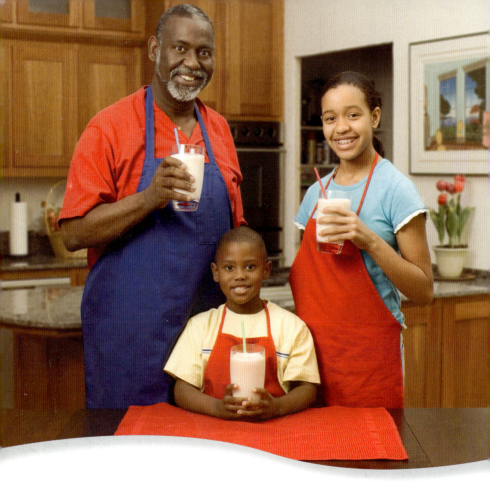

Mmm! We like smoothies.